You Look Beautiful in the Moonlight

a collection of
**Poetry, Prose,
Songs, and Plays**

by

Shelly Weinberg

You Look Beautiful in the Moonlight

Published by S&S Press
ISBN-13: 978-1975961718

This book is dedicated to my wife, Suzy, who brings beauty, love, and happiness to every day of my life.

This book would not have been possible without the help, support, and encouragement of Claudia McGhee, Paula Bernstein, Tom Nicotera, Charlie Chase, and my wife, Suzy Lamson.

Table of Contents

Introduction

I was first introduced to poetry through song lyrics: Cole Porter, Larry Hart, Johnny Mercer, Comden and Green, Alan Jay Lerner. Their work was funny, clever, inventive, sometimes poignant, often containing wonderfully original rhymes. When I read poetry I started with Ogden Nash whose style was unique and a delight — false rhymes, broken rhythms, and sometimes, perfect rhymes and perfect rhythms, and always clever and funny. I read Dorothy Parker, whose poems were witty, ironic, so perfectly written that I felt they should be cast in bronze. I read A. E. Housman and Thomas Gray, their poetry often broke my heart. I read rhythmic poetry: Longfellow, Robert Service — their rhythms picked me up and carried me away. Edgar Lee Masters and Pablo Neruda — their writing was a revelation. More recently, I listened to and then read the Performance Poets, Jack McCarthy, Patricia Smith, and Roger Bonair-Agard, whose writing and performance opened my eyes to what poetry could be.

All of these writers influenced my writing, whether it be poetry, prose, songs, or plays.

I had one other influence — my mother. When I was young, six, eight, ten, my mother would sing songs to me and tell me jokes. I grew up singing songs and telling jokes. Later, I started writing songs and making up jokes. And so, many of the pieces I included in this book are intended to be funny, to amuse you, the reader, the way my mother's jokes amused me.

Thanks, Mom, for showing me how.

Poetry

I've been told that I should organize these poems according to some basic organizational principle. But I couldn't find one. With the exception of a few love poems they came about at random. So I decided to present them to you in an order that seems reasonable to me, together with some comments that explain how the poems came about. I hope you enjoy them.

Hester's Disappointment

Author's Note

I don't remember why, but I decided to write a parody of The Scarlet Letter. I had never read the book so all I knew about the plot was that Hester Prynne had an affair with Arthur Dimmesdale — she had a child but she wouldn't reveal the name of the father — the townspeople were outraged — to shame her they forced her to wear a scarlet A on her clothing to indicate that she was an adulteress. That was all I needed to know about the story.

Hester Prynne was disappointed.
All that work ...
All those evenings
with Arthur Dimmesdale
studying
and whatever
culminating
in an all-nighter
and now
in front of her
her exam paper
and at the top
in red
a
B.

Hester looked up:
"Keep your grade.
I wouldn't take an A
if you gave me one."

Me and Camels Are Through

Author's Note

This poem was a gift. I was standing in line at a 7-11. The man at the front of the line ordered a pack of Camels. The man behind him said "You know, that's not really a Camel. That's a Dromedary." The man in front grunted, took his cigarettes and left. I stood there and thought: Wait a minute. You can't just ignore that. You have to reply. But, what? I spent the next two hours shopping and talking to myself. "That's not really a Camel. That's a Dromedary." By the time I got home, the poem was done.

I went to 7-11 the other day to buy a pack of Camels.

The fella behind me said:
"You know, that's not really a Camel. That's a Dromedary."

Well,
I thought I'd been smoking Camels for twenty years,
and now it turns out they lied to me.
I've been smoking Dromedaries.

And I don't know why I would want to smoke either one.
They're both mean, ill-tempered animals.
They spit at you and have an awful stink.

I thought: The next time I smoke a cigarette,
I'm not gonna smoke a Camel, or a Dromedary, or a Yak.
I'm gonna smoke an animal that's more like me.
Something that matches my character.

So I went back to 7-11 and bought a pack of
Sloths.

The Surgeon

Author's Note

I've had a few surgeries recently and I'm very impressed with the skill of the surgeons. How do they get to be that good? How do they practice? Maybe they start out doing surgeries on something other than people. Something like this.

I've developed an interest in surgery. It takes a lot of practice, so I've been honing my skills on barbecued chickens.

I'm getting good at the cutting apart phase.
Of course, surgeons eventually have to sew things back together.
I haven't tried that yet. I may have to delegate it.
The way they do on TV. "Doctor, close the patient up."

I'm preparing myself for that unforeseen crisis when someone calls out: "Is there a surgeon here?" I will step forward confidently and say: "I'm a surgeon. Has the patient been barbecued yet?"

Near Vanna

Author's Note

I never watch game shows. From time to time I've wondered — who watches these shows? I know they're very popular, but why? So one day I watched "Wheel of Fortune". It's a very charming show and I can see why it's lasted for more than a decade. Still, I imagined that somewhere there's a lonely man who sits at home day after day watching it and dreaming.

It's lonely
Sitting at home
Each afternoon
My only companion is my TV

While I watch game shows
I dream of her
Her blonde hair
Caressing her cheek

I imagine I'm there
With her
On stage
And she looks at me
Her eyes asking me a question
I smile at her
We move toward each other
Our hands touch
I watch her lips as she asks
"What letter would you like?"
I look into her eyes
As I say
"U"

Poet Laureate

Author's Note

Very often a poet laureate is an academic, someone who teaches at a well-known university. So I was pleasantly surprised to hear that some state or city or municipality had chosen as poet laureate a factory worker who wrote beautiful poetry.

O give me a poet laureate
Who's a regular kind of a guy.
A fella who'll buy you a beer or two
And help make the night go by.

And when the evening is growing late
And the drinking and chat have ended,
He's the guy who will drive you home
Though his license has been suspended.

The Iliad (revised)

Author's Note

Most people do not consider the limerick to be a serious poetic form. But what if it was a limerick with several hundred stanzas? On a classical theme? Such as The Iliad?
That sounded pretty good to me. So I set out to rewrite The Iliad in limerick form. Well, it turned out to be much more difficult than I imagined. I only have four stanzas so far. So, let's consider this a work in progress.

There once was a fellow from Ilium
Not Hector, not Harold, not Willium
T'was Paris, the cad
That oversexed lad
Who altered the fate of a millium.

Moaned Hector, What, me fight Achilles?
The thought of it gives me the willies.
He's strong as an ox
And sly as a fox.
By tonight I'll be covered with lilies.

Oh Father dear, don't be so thick.
Your stupidity makes me feel sick.
I've been saying for weeks
That it's filled up with Greeks.
That big wooden horse is a trick!

We all knew it would have to end one day.
Then they opened the gates on a Sunday.
When they rolled in the horse,
The Greeks jumped out, of course.
It was Sic Transit Gloria, Monday.

Rhyming

Author's Note

There's a special pleasure in rhyming.

June Moon
with Macaroon

I found my love
on Tishabov[1]

And yesterday I realized I could rhyme
Menelaus with
payus[2].

Well, that quickly gave rise to:

A Whole New View of the Iliad.
or
Who Knew He's A Jew?

Tell me, who are those guys on the dais ?
Why that's Paris and Reb Menelaus.
Now, the goy is from Troy,
But the orthodox boy
Is the one with the beard and the payus.

---

[1] A Jewish Holiday. I don't remember what it's about.
[2] Long curly sideburns worn by Ultra-Orthodox Jews.

Peter Goodman, Dentist, Hits It Big
or
On First Looking Into Homer Chapman

Author's Note

I was walking in the park when the name of the poem "On First Looking into Chapman's Homer" popped into my head. I had read the poem in high school, but I couldn't remember what the poem was about. I knew that Keats had written it, but that was all. I thought: this sounds like a medical exam. A doctor examining a patient named Chapman Homer or Homer Chapman. When I came home I found the poem and read the first line. "Much have I travelled in the realms of gold". I thought: It's not a doctor, it's a dentist! But it was neither. It's about Keats' great joy in reading Chapman's translation of the Iliad. As I read the poem I thought: this is a pretty good poem but it could use some improvement. And who would be more appropriate to rewrite it than me? After all, he's Keats and I'm Shelly.

Much have I dabbled in the realms of gold
And many a mouth of fillings have I spied
But never did I dream I would behold
The view when Homer Chapman opened wide.

When Homer Chapman opened up his mouth
A fortune beckoned from between his ears.
Why ev'ry single tooth is headed South !
I'll bet he hasn't flossed in forty years.

Oh, I could buy a Lexus if I choose !
"Eight implants here and crowns – I figure – ten !"
And also take a Caribbean cruise.
"Nurse, write it down and add it up again."
I couldn't wait to tell my wife the news,
Smiling at our home in Darien.

Have a good day

Author's Note

I'm Jewish. I was born in 1933. When World War II ended in 1945, the horror of the holocaust was revealed. I remember it vividly. But Jews aren't the only people who have experienced genocide: the Armenian genocide, the Rwandan genocide. And then horrors that were not man-made: Earthquakes, Fires, Tornadoes, Floods, those kinds of events that insurance companies like to call "Acts of God". Always we're left with the question: How does God allow this to happen?

I tried to ask this in a softer way, but without letting God off the hook.

We thank you, O Lord
for the glowing sunsets,
for the redwood forests,
for the deep red roses.
You created the snow-capped mountains, O Lord,
and for this we thank you.
Of course you created the Holocaust,
but everyone has a bad day,
now and then.

We thank you, O Lord
for the starlit heavens,
for the moonlit gardens,
for the fragrant flowers.
You created the night aurora, O Lord,
and for this we thank you.
Of course you created the Armenian Genocide,
but everyone has a bad day,
now and then.

We thank you, O Lord
for the sunlit rainbows,
for the Springtime blossoms,
for the Autumn colors.
You created the endless beaches, O Lord
and for this we thank you.
Of course you created the floods that drowned a million in
Bangladesh,
but everyone has a bad day,
now and then.

You created the giraffe, O Lord
and for this we thank you.
You created the butterfly, O Lord
and for this we thank you.
You created the jacaranda tree, O Lord
and for this we thank you.
O Lord …
Have a good day.

To Sharon Olds

You said you had written a poem but you didn't like it
more than once
poems that weren't good enough
so you put them away

I thought:
how nice to be that wealthy
to have so much disposable income
to buy clothing that you never wear

I thought of my notebook full of tatters
a stanza here
an opening line
a title
a phrase
an idea

The last time I finished a poem I was so elated
that I looked at it with loving eyes
and bonded with it
No editing for me
I loved it as it was
and hoped it would love me

Of course we can't all be wealthy
We learn to live within our means
It's a lesson that life teaches us

Yesterday I went to the store and bought a shoe
I'm saving my money
If all goes well
next month I'll buy the other

The Music Critic Reminisces

Author's Note

Some topics are irresistible. Rewriting Hamlet. Rewriting the Bible. And the subject of this poem.

Yes, I knew him.
He was wonderful.
A legend.
His playing was a revelation.
The colors – the textures.
He could have been the finest musician of his time.
His improvisations were without peer.
Sometimes they sparkled like a midnight sky.
Other times they thundered.
And he was not just a pianist.
He could play half a dozen instruments
with astonishing skill.
He had wonderful hands and an amazing ear.

Then, that unfortunate incident.
He was never the same.
And he knew it.
It ended his career.
He turned to painting.
It was a natural choice.
He was, after all, an artist.
And those hands, those fingers, that imagination.
Now people remember Van Gogh as a painter.
But oh, what he might have been.

The Hunter

Author's Note

*We had mice in our basement. Our friend, Linda, said: "I'll get them!"
And sure enough, she did. I considered printing up an impressive
looking certificate to acknowledge her achievement, but then, since
Linda is a poet, I decided a poem would be better.*

It was Hemingway that got me started.
I was captivated by the thought of it —
Big Game Hunting.
I read everything I could find,
went to sleep dreaming about it.
I rehearsed it in my mind.
As I grew older, I planned for it,
I saved for it, and then one day
I did it.

At first I was intoxicated by the experience.
The hunt.
The smell of the jungle.
But after a while, I realized that something was missing.
The challenge.

Shooting a rhino is like shooting an SUV.
How can you miss?
There's no subtlety to it.
I began to look for smaller prey,
more agile prey, smarter prey.
And the weapons were wrong.
The rifle, the shotgun.
They were too crude.
You might as well throw dynamite at the beasts.

Now I choose my prey thoughtfully.
I choose my weapon carefully.
This is to be a battle of wits,
a game of chess between two worthy opponents.

This week I bagged three mice!
They were fast, but their speed did them no good.
They were clever, but I was cunning.

I put out some bait.
As they approached, I turned on a bright light on the right,
a loud noise on the left, and then three of them were in my net!

I carried them to the woods, put out some food for them, and
released them.
I waved goodbye to them and turned and left.
We all knew who won.

Of course, I didn't catch all of them. Some of them got away.
They weren't fooled by my diversions.
That's the way it is when you have a worthy opponent.
It's never one-sided.

Tonight I will go to sleep and dream of the next hunt.

**String Theory
or
A Unified
"Theory of Everything"
combining
Quantum Theory
Relativity Theory
and
Laundry Theory**

Author's Note

*I'm a mathematician by training, but I've also studied a lot of physics.
I've spent a good deal of my professional life wondering about two
questions.
1- Why does the physical universe behave the way it does?
2- Where are my socks?
I believe the answer lies below.*

String Theory hypothesizes
a ten-dimensional space-time continuum
containing the usual
four dimensions
plus six additional dimensions
too small to be noticed
but large enough
for a single sock
to slip through

The Survivalist goes to Stop and Shop
a villanelle

Author's Note

I decided to write a villanelle. Not something glorious like Dylan Thomas' poem. I thought I would lower the bar. How about a so-so, mediocre, somewhat OK villanelle? That seemed achievable.

Do not drive slowly in the parking lot.
Quick, turn! We haven't got all day.
Fight, fight for that last elusive spot!

Those who win – the ones who know what's what —
why, they never hesitate. They
do not drive slowly in the parking lot.

See that man with the walker in that slot?
Push him out – that's not a place to stay.
Fight, fight for that last elusive spot!

That woman there, with the tiny little tot —
hit the horn — gives them time to move away.
Do not drive slowly in the parking lot.

Stay alert, and show them what you've got.
Cut him off – that rusty Chevrolet.
Fight, fight for that last elusive spot!

"After you"? That's fine for Camelot.
Get there first! That's why I always say:
Do not drive slowly in the parking lot.
Fight, fight for that last elusive spot!

What the Pig was Thinking

inspired by the painting "Porky in a Pickup"
by Del-Bourree Bach

Author's Note

The Courtyard Gallery in Mystic invited poets to participate in an ekphrastic poetry event. It's an event where poets write a poem about a painting or a sculpture in the gallery. I saw a painting that resonated with me. It showed a beautiful pink pig in the back of a pickup truck. I decided to write a persona poem, that is, a poem in the voice of a character, but there were no people in the painting. The only character in the painting was the pig. So I thought about the pig and waited. Two nights later I woke up in the middle of the night and the pig was talking to me. I went to the computer and typed it up as fast as I could.

First Maryanne washed me and brushed me so I glistened
and we walked over to the SUV
but my body never did fit into the back seats
and we never could manage the seat belts
so we went to the pickup truck
and Maryanne's dad took some lumber
and he built a ramp up to the back of the pickup truck
and I walked up the ramp slowly and carefully
until I finally got into the back of the pickup
and Maryanne's dad had spread blankets all over the truck bed
so I wouldn't get bruised while we were traveling
and Maryanne and her dad got into the truck
and Maryanne was dreaming of the fair and winning blue
ribbons

and I lifted my snout up into the warm sun
and the wind was blowing my ears around
and I felt like I was riding in a convertible with the top down
and I thought of Humphrey Bogart in Casablanca
that scene where he was driving through Paris in a convertible
and I imagined I'm hearing As Time Goes By on the radio
and I'm thinking
Hang on Ingrid I'm on my way!

Temple Beth Buy

Author's Note

I was driving home when suddenly I imagined a combination synagogue and electronics store called Beth Buy. That seemed like a funny idea but what could I do with it?

The commandment tells us:
Thou Shalt Not Covet Thy Neighbor's Wife,
And, of course, I would never do that.
It is wrong.
But still, did you see the screen on his new TV?
It's long and slim,
With two large speakers in front
And two small shapely ones in back.
When it was turned on
I couldn't take my eyes off it.
And when I heard the sound,
I confess, it made me tremble.

The commandment tells us:
Thou Shalt Not Steal,
And, of course, I would never do that.
It is wrong.
But still, did you see the price on that new laptop?
It's almost half the price of last year's model.
And then, those rebates —
It wouldn't take much on my part,
And it could be mine.

The commandment tells us:
Thou Shalt Not Use The Name Of The Lord In Vain,
And, of course, I would never do that.
It is wrong.
But still, did you see the new iPod Nano?
It's so thin and light.
It's as if it isn't there.
It's a miracle.
And the sound — it's heavenly.
Oh my G...

The Old Fashioned Way

Author's Comment

I went to a poetry event where some of the poetry was so abstract that I couldn't understand it at all. I decided to write a persona poem about a grouchy old poet who is always complaining that they don't write poetry the way they used to. However when it was finished, it didn't seem to be what I wanted it to say. I looked it over and decided that this was the voice of a romantic poet who misses the old-fashioned way of writing poetry. I changed the end, changed the title, and found it much more satisfying.

You know,
when I was young
people used to dance
the waltz
and the fox trot
and the rhumba
and they would hold each other
and move together
and look into each other's eyes.

But they don't do that anymore.
They get out onto the floor
and they do their own thing
to who-knows-what rhythm
that only they can hear
and you can't tell who's dancing with who.

Well, the same thing's happened to poetry.
Nobody cares about meter and rhyme anymore.
Nowadays people write poems and the words go their own way
and the words don't even hold hands
let alone dance cheek to cheek.

I remember when ...

>the two of us would walk along a stream
>and smile and laugh and chase a teen-age dream
>and spend the afternoon in carefree bliss
>and say goodbye that ended with a kiss

but poets today are off watching a sunset with their eyes closed
or racing down some road to a distant metaphor.

I just don't get it.
Where's the romance in that?

The poet hums a tune, "The Old Fashioned Way", and begins to dance.

Watching the sunset with my eyes closed

we arrived just before sunset
my wife and I
at the beach
in Carmel
in 1974

the sunset fan club had gathered
more than twenty of them
seated on the sand
waiting for today's performance

we joined them
sat in the back
I closed my eyes

I felt the warmth of the setting sun on my face
listened to the gulls flying by
tasted the salt air
probed the warm sand with my toes

when the sun descended below the horizon
the fan club applauded
someone shouted "do it again"

it was a beautiful day
that my wife and I shared
together

three years later she was gone
off to watch sunsets
with someone else

You Look Beautiful In The Moonlight

Author's Note

This is a poem or perhaps a play.
It's written in four voices.
It consists entirely of dialog.

The voices are:
Laurie and David — a young married couple
Rita and Harry — David's parents

Laurie and David were making love — then his cellphone rang

Don't answer it.
Yes, but… It's my mother.
Don't answer it.
But she might be sick… or injured… why would she call this
    late?
She's fine. Don't answer it.
Hello, Mom? Are you alright?
I'm fine.
Is Dad alright?
He's fine.
Then why are you calling me?
David, it's your cousin Murray. He's been in an accident.
I'm sorry to hear that. Is he OK?
He's fine, but his car was totaled.
That's too bad, but why are you calling me?
I want you to call him.
Mom, it's 11:30!
You don't have to call him tonight. Call tomorrow.
OK, but why do I have to call him?
You know he likes you and he feels so bad about the accident.
    Maybe you can cheer him up.

(Harry, what are you doing?)

(Rita, enough with the phone call. Hang up.)

(Harry, I'm on the phone with David.)

OK, Mom I'll call him tomorrow. Is that what you wanted to talk to me about?

(Rita, hang up. I want to talk to you.)

Yes. Thank you, David. I'm glad that you and Laurie are fine. I'll talk to you tomorrow.

Good night, Mom.

What did you want to talk about?

Rita, you look beautiful in the moonlight.

Harry, we're indoors — there is no moonlight.

There's moonlight somewhere — and Rita, you look beautiful.

That's sweet, Harry. What brought this on?

It's love, Rita. It's love.

Harry, you've been snacking on those little blue pills, haven't you?

They're only an aid. It's love, Rita.

Harry, come closer… and kiss me.

So, what did your mother want?

I don't know. I think she has nothing to do and she stays up late and invents reasons to call me.

Well, where's your father?

He's probably watching television or something.

Well, David, that was nice… while it lasted.

I got distracted.

And now?

Laurie, you look beautiful in the moonlight.

David, you look so handsome… in the moonlight.

About Love

Author's Note

When I came home at 3AM, the night I met Suzy, I wrote this poem.

I want to see the taj mahal
jewel encrusted birds
embedded in a marble ceiling
replicated a thousand times
built by a maharajah
as a testament of his love

I want to see the taj mahal
instead I went to dinner
ruthie and ruth and bob
and debbie and peter
and michael
and suzy
we dined and chatted
and suzy read her poetry
and we talked all night

I want to see the taj mahal
perhaps I have

Last Lines of a Poem

Author's Note:

Sometimes the last lines come first
and we work our way backwards
through the poem
as if through a maze
to a satisfactory beginning
so the poem seems to be of one piece.

That wasn't the case here.
I wrote the lines.
A few days later
I looked at them again
and decided
that I had what I wanted.

and last night
lying in bed
beside you
seeing your eyes
smiling at me
I was overwhelmed
by the desire
to take you in my arms
and kiss you
until the sun came up

One More Time

Author's Note

This poem is for my wife, Suzy.
Every time I do a reading, I like to end with this poem.

Had we but world enough and time
and I still had the energy,
no hill would be too hard to climb.
I'd come to you on bended knee
and ask you for your love this day.

But now my knees are hard to bend
and hills are now too much to climb.
My springtime years are at an end,
but still I come here one more time,
and ask you for your love this day,
and ask you for your love
this day.

Love Poem

For Suzy

Today in the last year of my life
I am embraced by happiness
As we cuddle each other
As we turn and smile
As we laugh together
As we make the bed together
As we stop in passing to kiss
And pause to say "I love you"
As we read to each other
As we hold each other
And press our cheeks together
As we play and laugh and smile and touch
I am filled with gratitude
That you are here
And that we can enjoy this day
Together

Prose

This section contains a wide assortment of writing. Short stories, even shorter stories, opera revisions, letters, political commentary, essays about scientific units, computer system design, poetry contests, Jewish holidays, and the death of friends.

Much of it is funny. Some of it is poignant. Some of it is very sad.

A Letter to the Poets

Many of you are wonderful poets and you've received much well-deserved praise for your skills, but, let's face it — none of you make money from your poetry. But you could.

When I was in college, Lipton Soup ran a poetry contest with a $10,000 first prize. Think about that. Ten thousand dollars!

Of course the kind of poetry they wanted wasn't your kind of poetry. They wanted a limerick. A limerick that began with: "Lipton Soups are the best".
I entered. I was very confident. I'm good at limericks. My entry was:

Lipton Soups are the best
They're hearty and fill you with zest
They're chock-full of flavor
You really will savor
And they're easy to wipe off your vest

I didn't win. I was very disappointed. But I took it as a challenge. I knew if I wanted to win the next contest, I'd have to hone my craft. And I did.

Now fifty years have passed and poetic styles have changed. People seldom write limericks any more. Most poetry today doesn't rhyme at all. It's written in free verse, often lyrical, and rich in imagery and metaphor.

That's the kind of poetry that you write. Lipton Soups knows that. So when they run the next poetry contest (with a $10,000 prize) that's the kind of poem that they'll ask for. So get ready. Start writing. I'm ready. I've written my entry.

34

Lipton soups take you to an earlier time
when you first fell in love
when you saw her approaching you
and as you ran toward her, her eyes sparkled
and as you embraced,
you felt the softness of her cheek against yours
and her hair smelled like
onion soup

Now that's a winning entry!

A Bronx Story

I grew up in the Bronx.
People in the Bronx are very skeptical.
And for good reason.
Because people in the Bronx lie a lot.
A lot of people in the Bronx lie a lot.
What's interesting is —
They don't lie for gain.
They lie for practice.
Lying is a skill and they don't want to lose their touch.
Which is why people in the Bronx are so skeptical.

So if you tell some people from the Bronx a story that seems to
drift into the world of fantasy, they give you that look...
And if you continue they ask you questions like:
"Were you there?"
(Eye-witnesses are big in the Bronx.)
"Were you there?"
And if you give them some lame answer like:
"No I wasn't — but my friend's brother knows somebody who
swears this is true."
Then they really give you that look and they tell you:
"Get outta here with that story"
and they walk away
and you've lost them.

All of which is why
the traditional Creation story never made it big in the Bronx.
I mean, people didn't arrive until the sixth day.
So how do you know what happened on the first five days?
And no matter what you tell them,
they give you that look.
and they ask you:
"Were you there?"
And no matter what you say, you've lost them.

And the Big Bang story of Creation doesn't do any better.
I mean, billions of years passing and space dust coalescing into
stars, and then galaxies, and planets forming, and life
appearing, and finally people.

That's when they give you that look
and they ask:
"Billions of years before people appeared — How do you know
what happened?"
And no matter what you say, they say:
"Were you there?"
And you've lost them.

Nevertheless,
there is a Creation story that has been handed down for
generations in the Bronx.
In the Bronx creation story, people were there from the
beginning.
That's how we know what happened.

We don't where the people came from.
We don't know where all this happened.
What we do know is there were people
and it was very dark.
We don't know what the people looked like.
It was too dark to see them.
But we could hear their voices.

There were four voices:
Voice # 1,
Voice # 2,
Murray,
and
Voice # 4.

In the beginning it was very dark, and silent.

After a while, Voice # 1 said:
"It's dark."

And Voice # 2 said:
"Yeah, it is dark."

And Voice # 1 said:
"I think it's darker than yesterday.
Do you think it's darker than yesterday?"

And Voice # 2 said:
"I dunno.
Yesterday was pretty dark.
Hey Murray, do you think it's darker than yesterday?"

And Murray said:
"Dark is dark!"

And then there was a very, very, very long silence.
Even longer than that.

And then Voice # 4 said;
" I got an idea!"

And Voice # 1 said:
"What? What's the idea?"

And Voice # 4 stood up and said:
"Let there be light!"

And there was light!
Everywhere!

The whole world glowed with light!

And Voice # 1 said:
"Woooooooooooooooooooooow!!!"

And Voice # 2 said:
"Ooooooooooooooooooooooh!!!"

And Voice # 1 said:
"He is smart!"

And Voice # 2 said:
"He's a leader!
We should follow him!"

And then there was a long silence.

Finally, Voice # 1 said:
"Now that it's light, what do you wanna do?"

And Voice # 2 said:
"I dunno.
Hey Murray, now that it's light what do you wanna do?"

And Murray said:
"I'm gonna take a nap.
Wake me up when it's dark."

Well, that's the story.
Now I know what you're thinking.
Was I there?

Well, of course I wasn't there.
It was a long time ago.

But, my friend's brother knows somebody who swears that this
is true.

Think it over.

Oedipus Rex

A while back I was chatting with one of my friends who lives in New York and he said, "What are you doing tonight?"

And I said, "Nothing much."

And he said, "I'm going to a cocktail party tonight. Lots of theater people. I know how interested you are in the theater and how much you enjoy it. Why don't you come with me."

So I went.

But when I got there I felt out of place, so I just stood in a corner of the room, drank some white wine, and listened. After a while I noticed another fellow standing on the periphery and I started talking to him.

"Do you go to many of these parties?"

"No. It's my first one."

"Are you in the theater?"

"Yes, I am."

"What do you do?"

"I'm a playwright."

"Really. Have you written anything that I might know?"

He smiled and said, "Not yet, but you will. I'm working on my first big play."

"What's it about?"

And he started telling me about his play. As he spoke his face lit up and he became more and more animated.

"It takes place in Greece a long time ago. Greece was divided into city-states and each city-state was ruled by a king. The play is about a young man who has a dream about his destiny. He believes that it is his destiny to become a king — the king of the great city of Thebes.

"Now, he doesn't live in Thebes. He lives in the mountains far away. And he believes that in order to become a king, he must become a great warrior — a warrior that no one can defeat.

"So that's what the first act is about. His dream, his destiny, how he becomes a warrior, a great warrior. How he challenges other warriors and defeats all of them.

"Finally he realizes that he is ready. Ready to go to Thebes and become Oedipus (that's the hero's name), Oedipus the King. Oedipus Rex. And that's the title of the play, Oedipus Rex."

I didn't know what to say. I felt a bit awkward but I finally said "Oedipus Rex has been written."

He got very upset. "Who, who wrote my play? Who wrote Oedipus Rex?"

I said, "Ever hear of Sophocles?"

He became angry. "Hey, don't talk down to me. Of course I've heard of Sophocles. Everybody's heard of Sophocles. Greek, right? Owns a diner."

I tried to smile. "Yeah, that's him."

"So this Sophocles fella, when did he write Oedipus Rex?"

"Twenty-five hundred years ago."

He looked at me coldly. His eyes narrowed. And he said "They all say that." And then he turned and walked away.

I felt like I had really put my foot in my mouth. I had made him angry, insulted him. I ran after him to apologize.

"Hey, wait a minute, this happens often in the theatre. Two people write different plays with the same title. I'm sure your Oedipus Rex is different from the one that Sophocles wrote."

"You bet it's different."

"Why don't you tell me more about it. It sounds like a really interesting play."

The smile came back to his face. And he began to tell me more about the play.

"The second act is all about how Oedipus travels to Thebes and the adventures that occur along the way. He meets another warrior on the road and the warrior commands Oedipus to stand aside. But Oedipus will not stand aside. Oedipus knows that he is destined to be a king. So they do battle and Oedipus kills the other warrior.

"Well, there are many more adventures until Oedipus finally arrives at Thebes. Now Thebes is a walled-city and there is only one way to get in and out of the city and that is through the Great Gate of Thebes. But Thebes has a curse on it. And no one can enter or leave the city because the Great Gate is guarded by a terrifying creature, half-animal — half-human, that is called the Sphinx. Now, like I said, the Sphinx is terrifying. It's ten feet high and has the body of a lion and the head of Margaret Thatcher.

"But Oedipus is not terrified. Oedipus is fearless. Oedipus approaches the Sphinx and the Sphinx says 'Where are you going?'

"And Oedipus says, "I'm going to enter Thebes."

"And the Sphinx says, 'You can enter Thebes, but first you must answer my riddle. But if you answer incorrectly, you will die.'

"Now Oedipus doesn't know anything about riddles. He's never heard a riddle. But Oedipus is fearless. And he says, 'What's the riddle?'

"And the Sphinx smiles and says, 'What walks on four legs in the morning, two legs at noon, and three legs in the evening?'

"Oedipus has never heard anything like this. He's baffled but he knows that nothing can stop him. Finally his face lights up and he says, 'I've got it. A herring.'

"The Sphinx says, 'A herring?'

"Oedipus says, 'A herring!' "

I said, "A herring?"

The playwright said, "A herring!"

I said, "You put the herring joke in Oedipus Rex?"

The playwright said, "It works. It's beautiful. Just listen.

"Where was I? Oh, yeah, the riddle. The Sphinx says, 'What walks on four legs in the morning, two legs at noon, and three legs in the evening?'

"Oedipus says, 'A herring.'

"The Sphinx says, 'A herring doesn't walk on four legs in the morning.'

"Oedipus says, 'But you could put four legs on it.'

"The Sphinx says, 'A herring doesn't walk on two legs at noon.'

"Oedipus says, 'So you could take two legs off.'

"The Sphinx is beginning to see where this is headed and she doesn't like it, but she says, 'A herring doesn't walk on three legs in the evening.'

"And Oedipus says, 'So you could put one leg back on.'

"And the Sphinx gets very angry but doesn't say anything. Finally the Sphinx says, 'I never thought of that.' And the Sphinx says, 'Alright. You can enter Thebes and you can sleep with whoever you like and you can kill whoever you like but don't make trouble.'

"Oedipus smiles and walks past the Sphinx. The Great Gates of Thebes open. The people of Thebes who have been gathered on the ramparts cheer. The curse has been lifted. Oedipus enters Thebes in triumph as the curtain falls.

"What d'you think?"

"Well this sure is a different play. I love it."

"You like that ending?"

"It's great. It's one of a kind."

"I have another ending, maybe better than the first. Would you like to hear it?"

"Sure, I'd love to."

"OK, we're back at the riddle. The Sphinx says, 'What walks on four legs in the morning, two legs at noon and three legs in the evening?'

"Oedipus is baffled. Finally his face lights up and he says, 'I've got it. A heron.'

"The Sphinx laughs and says, 'No, you dummy, it's a herring. I knew you'd never get it.' And the Sphinx kills Oedipus. The people of Thebes gathered on the ramparts throw their hands up in despair. The curse remains. The curtain falls on Act II.

"What d'you think?"

"You killed Oedipus in Act II?"

"Yeah, what d'you think?"

"You killed the hero in Act II? What are you going to do in Act III?"

He looked at me and smiled. "Don't you get it? That's what the audience is going to say. They will never get up for the intermission. They will be glued to their seats — waiting to find out what's going to happen in Act III."

"Well, what is going to happen in Act III?"

He smiled and said "I have a few ideas."

"Now I really want to see this play. When did you say it's going to be finished?"

"Well, I figure about two months to finish the script. Then, I'll have to get a director, a cast for the read-through, a venue and we will have arrange for potential backers to see it. I figure the whole thing should take about five months."

I said, "Look, here's my card. Here's my cell phone number. I really want to see this play. Call me when it's ready to be seen."

Well, we chatted a bit longer. Then he had to leave. I haven't heard from him since. That was five months ago. I keep my cell phone on all the time. I really want to see this play.

Three New (Happy) Endings to Carmen

I went to see Carmen the other day. Great opera! But the last act is a downer.
Here's how it goes:

At the end of Act 3, Don Jose's life is in ruins. Don Jose has deserted from the army to be with Carmen. He has abandoned his sweetheart Micaela. He is a fugitive, living in the mountains with a gang of smugglers.

But Carmen has tired of Don Jose. She is attracted to the toreador, Escamillo.

Don Jose is jealous and threatens Escamillo. Suddenly, Micaela appears and tells Don Jose that his mother is dying. Don Jose and Micaela go back to his village to see his mother. As he departs, Jose warns: "I'll be back."
The curtain falls on Act 3.

Pretty heavy stuff, setting up the tension in Act 4.

Act 4 – Bizet's Version

Escamillo and Carmen arrive at the bullring in Seville.

Escamillo leaves to prepare for the bullfight.

Don Jose emerges from the shadows. He tells Carmen he still loves her. He pleads with her to come back to him. Carmen rejects him. He threatens her.

Carmen tells Don Jose: "I am not afraid. I live my life my way".

Don Jose becomes enraged. He pulls a knife. He kills Carmen.

Don Jose bursts into tears.

(Note: Bizet missed an opportunity here. He should have had Don Jose sing the heartbreaking aria: "I have killed the woman I love".)

Anyway, the curtain falls and the opera ends.

Very dramatic and very exciting, but too tragic.
This opera could really use a happy ending.
So here are three new happy endings to Carmen.

Act 4 – The Hometown Girl Version
(Act 4 takes place in Don Jose's village)

Don Jose is moved by Micaela's love for him and her loyalty.

Don Jose sings the beautiful aria "I fell in love with the one next door".

Micaela sings the short but beautiful aria: "Me too".

Don Jose decides to build a new life, but first he must pay the price for deserting from the army. He turns himself in and is sent to prison.

Micaela sings the beautiful aria: "I will wait for you, but don't take too long".

There is a brief musical interlude as Don Jose serves two years in prison.

Don Jose comes out of prison and is met at the gate by Micaela, the priest, the caterer, and a large group of wedding guests.

Don Jose and Micaela are married and sing the beautiful duet: "This is a love worth waiting for".

There is another brief musical interlude indicating the passage of five or so happy years.

One day Carmen appears in the village. She turns and shouts to someone off-stage: "Hurry up Escamillo, you're always lagging behind".

Escamillo appears. He is limping and using a walker. He replies: "Yes dear".
He looks to the heavens in despair.

Don Jose watches this and sings the poignant aria: "What did I ever see in her".

He holds Micaela in his arms and sings (again) the beautiful aria: "I fell in love with the one next door".

Micaela sings an even shorter version of the beautiful aria: "Me too".

Don Jose and Micaela go off arm in arm as the curtain falls.

Act 4 – The Gay Version

Escamillo and Carmen arrive at the bullring in Seville.

Escamillo leaves to prepare for the bullfight.

Don Jose emerges from the shadows. He tells Carmen he still loves her. He pleads with her to come back to him. Carmen rejects him. He threatens her.
Carmen sings the dramatic aria: "No man can own me. I live my life my way".

Don Jose becomes enraged. He pulls a knife. But in his confusion, he has taken a butter knife. Carmen laughs at him and calls him a fool. Don Jose bursts into tears.

Escamillo emerges from the shadows.

Escamillo puts his arm around Don Jose and says: "Don't cry Jose, no woman is worth it. Come with me to my place. We'll have a drink together, and perhaps I can show you the true meaning of love."

Escamillo and Don Jose sing the beautiful duet: "I've found true love at last".

They go off arm in arm as the curtain falls.

Act 4 – The Vegetarian Version

Don Jose remains in his village with Micaela. We don't see them again.

Escamillo and Carmen arrive at the bullring in Seville.

Escamillo is about to enter the bullring when he stops and says: "I can't do it. I won't do it. Killing animals is wrong! I won't do it. The toreador's life has made me rich and famous, but it's over. I'm going to buy a farm in the countryside and grow vegetables. Carmen, you can stay here or come with me, but I'm going."

Carmen says: "A farm! I'd love to live on a farm. As a teenager I had dreams of a vegetable garden. Rows and rows of zucchini. I wonder what that meant?"

Then Carmen sings the beautiful aria: "My true love is a vegetable".

Carmen and Escamillo go off arm in arm as the curtain falls.

One Day at a Time

Tuesday, I went to have my blood drawn for a PSA.

Sitting in the waiting area in Medical Oncology, I looked at the people around me. All Cancer patients. An old black man with a white beard that contrasted beautifully with his skin. He sat quietly, a look of serenity on his face. A young woman with a worried look on her face, fidgeting in her chair. An old man, moving slowly, sitting down with difficulty. His wife, helping him, comforting him, reassuring him. As I left the Physician's Building I passed an elderly white-haired couple entering the lobby. That's what happens as we get older. Life brings us to the Physician's Building.

Passing the hot dog cart in front of the parking structure, I saw a woman with four children, buying hot dogs for them. The mother seemed busy, managing the transaction. The children, all smiling, were eating their hot dogs.

A woman passed by wheeling her baby in a stroller. She had a broad smile on her face. I imagined that she was smiling because of her joy and love for her child.

As I came to the door of the parking structure, it opened and a woman with two canes walked though very slowly. I held the door open for her and she smiled. She had great difficulty walking, but she smiled.

Perhaps that's what we were all doing: trying to get through the day as well as we can. Some of us old, some of us young, some of us worried, frightened, some of us happy — happy to be alive, happy to have children, happy to have a hot dog.

All of us living one day at a time.

The Big Reunion

I'm going in for surgery next month.
It's not a trivial surgery – it's pretty complex.
But I'm in pretty good health
and I checked it out with my doctors
and they all say I'm going to be OK

but there's always some risk
and you never know...

There's a certain amount of scare in it.
What if I don't make it.
What if I wake up ...
in heaven.
What's it going to be like?

The problem with heaven is
people are always talking about it
but they always leave out the details.
They never tell you the things you really want to know about.
It's all a lot of maybes.

Things like —
what do you wear?

Do you show up wearing the last thing that you wore?

Am I going to show up in a hospital gown that's open in the
back?
Is that how I'm going to be dressed in heaven?

Is that it?
An eternity of embarrassment?
It's got to be better than that.
Maybe you can pick what you wear.
I'm pretty comfortable in khakis
but maybe that's too informal.

How about a sweater and some slacks...
I like these running shoes – they're so comfortable
I hope people won't mind if I wear them.

Maybe it's not like that at all.
Maybe they give you something to wear
The men get one thing and the women get another thing
But they're all the same.

What if heaven is like that ?

It's sort of like going to a prom and everyone shows up wearing
the same thing.
What a nightmare that is when the women spent two months
picking out the perfect prom dress and everyone shows up
wearing the same dress.
It's funny the men don't seem to mind wearing the same thing.
Everyone shows up in a tuxedo.
You can still tell who's who.
It's not a problem.

Although, I really don't know.
I never went to the prom.
I didn't have a date.
So I don't know.

Maybe it's more like a reunion.
A big reunion.

And you get there and you see people you haven't seen in a
long time.
And you say
"Harry, is that you?
Gee, you used to have wavy hair – and now it's all gone."
Maybe it's like that.
You go around looking at people saying "Is that you?"

People say you'll meet your family —
Your mother.
I'd like to meet my mother.
I'd like to see her again.
She died thirty-nine years ago.
It's been a long time.
I'd like to see her.
She was the kindest person I've ever known.
I'm sure I must have irritated her lots of times.
But, I don't remember her being annoyed at me.
All I remember is her loving me
and forgiving me.
And that's what I've needed all my life —
someone to love me and forgive me.
Because I've never been perfect.

I'd like to see her
but I don't know how to find her.
How will I get in touch with her?
I'm sure they don't have cell phones up in heaven.
None of that high-tech stuff.
Or maybe they do.
They don't tell you.

Maybe every year they give them the latest smartphone.
"OK everybody. We know last year you all got the iPhone but a new phone has come out with a bigger screen and a better camera so we're taking the old ones back and giving you the new ones."
I can see all the people throwing their hands up in the air and saying:
"Hey, it took me a year to learn to use this one. Forget it. Do I have to take the new one?"

But maybe I'm underestimating them.
Maybe they like that stuff.
Maybe they're sitting around there taking pictures of each other.
Maybe my mother is saying
"Hey, Take a picture of me with my new smartphone.
I'll send it to my son. Boy, will he be surprised."

Can you picture that?
I wake up, turn on my cell phone, and there's a picture of my mother.
Now, that's a long distance call.

But, I don't think so.
Because I never did get a picture of my mother on my cell phone.

Maybe the way it works is they give you the kind of technology that you're used to.
So she has a phone that plugs into the wall.

I'll call her.
But, I don't even remember our old phone number.
I guess they must have information up there.

I wonder if she sits there waiting for my call.
Patiently. Saying "He said he'd call. But you know how kids are. They're always busy doing something. He'll call tomorrow."

No, Mom. I meant it. I'll call today. I'll call as soon as I get a phone and find your number. I want to see you, but how do I find you?

Is there a part of heaven that says — this is for people from the Bronx?

Is that where you go?
"Everybody from the Bronx gather around that tall tree."
That's a lot of people.
And how will I find her?
How will I recognize her?

I can picture going through a sea of little old ladies saying "Are you my mom?"

There are so many of them.
But she was pretty short.
Maybe if they lined in order of size like in school.
"OK. Everybody line up. Small ones in the front."
She was at most 5' 2" at her peak. Later in life she must have been 5 feet tall.
So I'll just look through the millions of 5 foot tall little old ladies.

Maybe she's looking for me.
Maybe she stands there at the New Arrivals every day asking;
"Is that my son?"

Maybe that's not how it works at all.

Maybe it's like that big reunion where everyone wears a name tag and you have a picture of yourself when you were younger.

How will I recognize her?
What if she doesn't look like she did when she was older.
What if she looks like she did when she was young?
When she was seventeen?

I never knew what she looked like then.

So maybe she would wear a picture of herself when she was older so I would recognize her.
And I'd wear a picture of myself
when I was six
and we went to the World's Fair
and they took a picture of me in my sailor suit.
I still have that picture.
She'd remember that.

And I'll wear a name tag
so she'll know it's me

I'll get one now
and I'll carry it with me so I'll always have it
And I'll put it on
and it will say...

"Hi Mom, I'm your son."

Hi
Mom,

I'm
your
son.

A Letter to my Friends

To my wonderful friends:

Thank you for all of your kind letters, thoughts, and good wishes.

Life is full of strange twists and turns.
Today is Suzy's birthday.
She's 64 years old.
She went to the gym this morning and worked out.
She did two miles on the treadmill.
She's faster than I am.
She had never been to a gym until two years ago when I brought her there.
Now she goes almost every day.

She went out to buy a package of chocolate chip cookies.
The man behind the counter at the post office is going through a difficult time.
Suzy is going to give him the cookies to cheer him up.
Suzy said that's her birthday present to herself. That act of kindness.

And I'm sitting here thinking how lucky I am to be married to this wonderful woman.
And to have friends like you.

Today, after she came home from the gym, Suzy, one year short
of Medicare, smiled and said: "I've become a jock."
It's true.
Suzy's become a jock.
And I've become a poet.

Who'd have imagined it?

My love to all of you, whatever you've become.

Shelly

The GUI Metaphor

You might be wondering what I've been doing lately, so I'll tell you — I've been thinking.

You see, I've been working on the design of an auto insurance system. This new system is going to be very, very easy to use.

The basic idea seems to be that you should design the screen, also known as the Graphic User Interface, or GUI (pronounced gooey), so that it shows you (meaning the insurance broker) a whole bunch of familiar objects in a familiar environment so that you will know what to do with them, intuitively, because they're so familiar. The GUI should be a metaphor for the way you work.

The way I'm picturing it is that you're an insurance broker and someone comes in to buy some auto insurance and you sit down in front of your screen and click and drag icons and put together their insurance policy. So if they want collision coverage, you drag the car icon from the toolbar, then you drag another car icon from the toolbar and smash it into the first car, and then the screen says "Collision". If they want personal injury coverage, you take the person icon and run it over with the car icon. If they also want coverage for accidental death, you take the person icon, which by now is bleeding pretty badly, and drop it into the casket icon. Your legal expenses are covered by the lawyer icon, and if he's not doing a satisfactory job you can always hit him with the car icon.

What I'm wondering is: Is dragging all these icons around really an improvement?

If you want to delete a file on the MAC, you take the file icon and drag it over to the garbage can icon and drop it in. Do we really need a garbage can icon? What's wrong with hitting the Delete key? I realize that some people don't like to let go of the mouse. So then pick up the mouse and hit the Delete key with it.

Microsoft just spent a lot a money designing what they think is a really friendly GUI metaphor for the workplace. To show how friendly it is they called it "Bob".
I've never met "Bob", but I read the PR and here's how it works, sort of. When you start up Bob, you get a picture of a real friendly workplace. Bob has a desk, and a library, and a phone, and a fax, and whatever else Bob needs. All of this is so familiar and so inviting that it should be child's play for anybody to sit down at the computer and do something productive. And it's all obvious. If you want to send a fax, you click on the fax icon.

What I want to know is this — if you want to take a break, how do you tell the computer? Do you click on the Bob icon and drag it to the toilet icon? And if you do that, and you get a phone call, will your voicemail answer: "I'm sorry, Bob is away from his desk right now, but he might be back in a few minutes, depending on whether or not he took the newspaper icon with him".

A Contract on America

Author's Note

I'm a Democrat. But I enjoy watching Republicans. They are often, intentionally or not, a great source of comedy. I wrote this piece in 1994 when the Republicans announced they would reduce the deficit by lowering taxes and increasing military spending. Well, it's now 2017 and once again the Republicans have announced that they will reduce the deficit by lowering taxes and increasing military spending. I think it involves invading Greenland.

I was reading the paper the other day, and noticed that Newt Gingrich and about 300 other Republicans in Congress have taken out a contract on America. Well, I don't know that a contract is really necessary. I mean, the Republicans have been doing their best to mess up the country for the last 14 years without a contract. These are dedicated people, these Republicans. When they say they're going to mess up the country, by golly, you know that you can count on them to do it.

And they're good at it.

For example, when Reagan was running against Carter, he made a point of needling Carter about the deficit. He talked a lot about fiscal responsibility, and things like that, and boasted that he could balance the budget by reducing taxes and increasing defense spending. They called it supply-side trickle-down charge-everything-on-your-credit-card-and-throw-away-the-bill economics.

But it didn't work.

The problem was, with all that wheeling and dealing that was going on in Washington, the Reagan team became confused and forgot their plan. Instead of throwing away the bill, they actually paid it. Well, you know the rest. In no time at all, the government was broke and they had to borrow a potfull of money to stay in business.

Now, I don't mean to oversimplify a complex subject. There was more to the problem than just having a bad memory — although Republicans are noteworthy for being good at having bad memories.

They tried lots of things. They reduced taxes to strengthen the economy. The deficit got bigger. So they raised taxes to strengthen the economy. The deficit got even bigger.

They adopted a strong dollar policy. Unfortunately, the strong dollar policy weakened the country. You see, the strong dollar made our products too expensive for other countries to buy. By 1984 the only things we were exporting successfully were old Ronald Reagan movies. So then they adopted a weak dollar policy.

That didn't work either. The only thing left to do was to take the country's mind off these financial matters.

So they invaded Grenada!

It was a brilliant stroke. Even though nobody had ever heard of Grenada, everybody loves a victory — and we had a victory. Even though it turned out that the number of reporters covering the story exceeded the population of Grenada, the public loved it.

It's worth noting, however, that even a tiny victory cannot be taken for granted. So the Reagan folks barred the press from Grenada for the first three days — just in case we lost.

Well, we did win after all and the diversion worked beautifully. It worked so well that the Reagan team came up with another spectacular diversion.

You see, by now the annual deficit was so large that the national debt had tripled! People were beginning to notice. So the Reagan folks needed something big. And they came up with a winner — The Iran-Contra Scandal.

As it always is with great ideas — it was simple. First they banned the sale of arms to Iran. Then they sold arms to Iran. They cut off funds for the Contras. Then they took the money from the sale of arms to Iran and used it to supply the Contras. Then, and this is the brilliant part, they leaked the story to the press!

It was fabulous. Everybody loved it. Congress held hearings and everybody watched them on TV all day and then watched the summaries at night. Nobody even noticed that the national debt had increased by another trillion dollars. Let's face it. Who, aside from a few anal-retentive accountants, is going to stay up nights checking the books when you can contemplate Fawn Hall smuggling secret documents out of the White House in her underwear?

Well, nobody ever talked about the deficit again — until last week.

Last week Newt Gingrich proposed a plan to cut the deficit by reducing taxes and increasing defense spending. He called it "A Contract on America". I don't know the details but I understand that step one is to invade Bermuda.

The (possibly true) Story of Chanukah

Author's Note

I'm sure many of you know the story of Chanukah. But It couldn't hurt to get a second opinion.

Many years ago, in the land of Judea, Judah Maccabee and his tribe were engaged in a great battle with their enemies, the Macaroons. The Maccabees defeated the Macaroons and came home to celebrate their victory. Judah Maccabee told his child, Julia, to prepare a dinner of latkas for the celebration. But she cried, "Alas, Father, there is only enough oil for one latka." "Well, then make it a big one", said Judah.

And it came to pass that Julia made a latka big enough to feed the entire tribe. And they went to bed contented.

The next morning Julia awoke and found that a miracle had occurred and the oil had not been depleted, so she made another giant latka for breakfast and fed the entire tribe once again.

And it came to pass that this miracle was repeated for eight days, and the tribe ate latkas for breakfast, lunch, and dinner for eight days.

On the ninth day, Judah Maccabee awoke and said, "I'm so full I can hardly move. What will I do if the Macaroons attack us?"

Wisely, Julia Maccabee advised, "Send a messenger to the Macaroons and offer to meet with them and make peace with them and share latkas with them."

And it came to pass that the Maccabees and the Macaroons met together and made peace together and the Maccabees brought latkas and the Macaroons brought small cakes made of almond paste and they shared these gifts with each other and there was peace for ever and ever (or until they got hungry again).

Each year to celebrate this miracle, the Maccabees held a Festival of Latkas which they named "Chanukah", but no one knows why.

The (possibly true) Story of Passover

Author's Note:

An early Jewish manuscript, including the only known text of what is known as the Story of Passover, has surfaced after 3,000 years. The text gives new insights into the relationship of Moses and the Pharaoh, scholars reported today. In this version, Pharaoh commands the Israelites to go.

The discovery in the desert of Egypt of this papyrus manuscript was announced by the National Theographic Society at a news conference in Washington. Ivory Vellum, an executive vice president of the Theographic Society, said the manuscript is considered by scholars and scientists to be the most significant ancient text to be found in the past 2 weeks.

"Although only a few fragments have been translated so far, they give us new insights into the Passover story" Mr. Vellum said. "This is absolutely typical of ancient Jewish manuscripts," said Stephen Munster, professor of Judaic studies at the University of Emmental in Switzerland. "I am completely convinced."

Fragments translated so far

Many years ago, in the land of Egypt . . .

One day Moses was walking through the desert and he saw a great forest fire burning in the desert.

And Moses said to himself: "A forest fire where there are no forests? This is indeed a miracle. But what can it mean?"

Just then a frog jumped in front of Moses and said: "Go to the Pharaoh and tell him: 'Let my people go'."

And Moses said to himself, "A talking frog in the middle of a desert? This is indeed a miracle. But what can it mean? I understand the message of the frog, but who listens to frogs?"

And Moses went to the palace of the Pharaoh and said: "I want to speak to the Pharaoh."

And the Pharaoh's minister said: "You may see the Pharaoh, but first you must put this white makeup on your face, and these long floppy shoes on your feet, and this red ball on your nose."

And Moses did as he was told. And Moses stood before the Pharaoh and said: "Let my people go."

And the Pharaoh said: "Who is this clown? Get rid of him."

And Moses cried out in frustration: "They won't listen to me. Punish them. Punish them and make them listen to me."

And a great plague of gingivitis came over the land of Egypt and it afflicted all of the male Egyptians.

Many plagues later . . .

And a great plague of diarrhea came over the land of Egypt and it afflicted all of the male Egyptians.

And Moses went to the palace of the Pharaoh and said: "I want to speak to the Pharaoh."

And the Pharaoh's wife said: "The Pharaoh is indisposed."

And Moses shouted out to the Pharaoh: "I know where you are. Let my people go."

And the Pharaoh shouted back: "You want to go? I can't stop going. I command that all of the Israelites go. (That'll teach them.)"

And Moses said: "Here's my plan. We will hotfoot it to the shore of the Red Sea. Then we will take the last ferry across the Red Sea to the endless desert on the other side. Then we will disembark and enter the endless desert. Then we will get lost."

And Moses' advisers said: "Good plan, but the ferry is very expensive, and to pay the fare for all of these people, we're gonna need a lot of bread."

And Moses told his people: "Bake bread! Hurry! We're leaving in an hour."

And the people said: "An hour? The bread won't have time to rise."

And Moses told his people: "Bread is bread. Just do it. If we miss the last ferry, we'll have to walk across the Red Sea."

And the voice said to Moses: "These are my commandments. I have carved them onto eight stone tablets. Take them to your people."

And Moses was very tired from climbing up the mountain. And Moses looked at the tablets and said to himself: "Tablets, shmablets, do I look like an octopus? I'll take these two and come back tomorrow for the rest."

Three Children's Stories

Author's Note:

I never knew any children's stories. I never had any children's books. We were poor. We couldn't afford them. Nobody ever read any children's stories to me.[3]
Somehow, I heard the story of Goldilocks and the Three Bears.

So, when I decided to write children's stories, the only model I had was The Three Bears. Which is why these three stories look the way they do.

---

[3] There's a happy ending here. When I married Suzy, she read Charlotte's Web to me. I wept when Charlotte died.

Story 1

Once upon a time in the village of Unter-finster-schwagen there lived three dwarfs: A great big papa dwarf, a cuddly medium sized mama dwarf (who could be quite assertive when she felt like it), and a cute little baby dwarf named Helga Sue.

The three dwarfs lived in a small cottage at the edge of the village near the Great Forest. In the Great Forest there was a cave which was the home of a sociopathic young woman who liked to break into houses. Because of her fondness for yellow dresses, the townspeople called her Goldifrocks.

Story 2

Once upon a time in a small village in The Ileum there lived 375,000 bacteria: A great big papa bacterium and 374,999 cute little baby bacteria. One day the papa bacterium went off to audition for a job on the stage (actually the third stage of digestion). The children called out with cries of encouragement.

"Good luck, papa."
"Break a cilium!"

Story 3

Once upon a time in a small village in The Great Clock there lived three minutes: A great big Papa Minute, a medium sized Mama Minute (who could be quite fast), and a cute little Baby Minute.

Every day they would take five and sit around and discuss philosophy. One day the Papa Minute stood up and announced solemnly:

"If my time is your time, then there must be minutes that are (h)ours!"

A Letter to Tina

Dear Tina,

Before I met you, I felt that we had been friends already.

I shared an office with Pat and Gene. One day you and Pat had a long telephone conversation. I listened as I worked. I never heard your voice – only Pat's half of the conversation. When it was over I asked Pat, "Who was that?" "That was Tina", she said.

In the months that followed I heard fragments of one-sided conversations. Without knowing any of the specifics, the tone of the conversations told me of the ups and downs of your life.

"How is Tina?"
"She's not feeling well."

"How is Tina?"
"She's much better."

There were many conversations filled with joy and laughter.
Pat told me that her family and yours had been close friends for many years.
As time went on I felt I knew you.

When we finally met, to me, it felt more like a reunion of old friends. You and Clyde were so easy to be with and made me feel so comfortable. I enjoyed your enthusiasm. I was impressed with your energy and your passion for cooking and your creativity and your remarkable knowledge of its history.

Most of all I enjoyed the closeness between you, Clyde, Pat, Jeff, Thomas, and Christopher. You were like one family. I felt privileged to be part of your family gatherings.

After Suzy and I moved to Connecticut, I called Pat from time to time. I would ask about you. One day the news came and it was not good. The doctors had found cancer and it had spread.

When I heard that the cancer had spread I hoped for something. I had lost a close friend to cancer twenty-six years ago. In those days there was no hope.
But now it's different. There is hope. So I hoped. I hoped for some treatment — some new drug that would shrink the tumor — stop its growth — make you comfortable — buy more time. I hoped for time.

Time for your birthday. Time for Suzy to meet you and Clyde. Time to sit and talk. Time for you to tell her about history and bread and wheat and how it changed civilization. Time to smile at each other. Time to laugh. Time.

It didn't work out that way.

I was shocked when I heard you were gone.

I was torn by my feelings.
I had wanted more time.
I was glad you were at peace.

I'm glad that your family and friends were with you — talking to you — comforting you — loving you.

You'll always be with us.

Goodnight Tina, and flights of angels sing you to your rest.

Shelly

Remembering Rosemary

I thought of Rosemary today, again. She was a close friend from IBM. She died in 1977, 40 years ago. I still think of her, often. She went into the hospital for a hysterectomy. When they opened her up they found cancer of the liver. It was inoperable. She wept when they told her and for many days afterwards. I went to see her in the hospital, and at home several times, and finally at the funeral. She was diagnosed in February. By Thanksgiving she was gone. She was 35 years old.

I still miss her.

When I hear the James Taylor song "Fire and Rain", it reminds me of her.

> *I've seen fire and I've seen rain*
> *I've seen sunny days that I thought would never end*
> *I've seen lonely times when I could not find a friend*
> *But I always thought that I'd see you again*

I still can't get used to Rosemary being gone.
But she is gone.
And all I'm left with is her memory and a tear.

Songs

I've been writing songs since I was a teenager. Sometimes the lyric and the melody — sometimes just the lyric using an existing melody. Most of them are lost. I saved a few of the recent ones.

Big Sadie's Blues

Author's Note

I received an email containing a piece of humor called "How to Sing the Blues". Very funny. Google it. You'll love it. It also explained how to write the blues. So I made up a tune and wrote this song.

Took my man to Memphis
and then I shot him there.
Yes, I took my man to Memphis
and then I shot him there.
We was shoppin' for a couch –
now I'm gonna get the chair.

Went into a bar
to get my man a Coke.
Yes, we went into a bar
to get my man a Coke.
He took one look at the waitress
and my couch went up in smoke.

Sent me for a walk
so he could have some fun.
Yes, he sent me for a walk
so he could have some fun.
I walked back to the truck
and got myself a gun.

Ran back to the bar to
tell my man that we was through.
Yes, I ran back to the bar to
tell my man that we was through.
He was lovin' up that waitress
So I knew jus' what to do.

Shot him in the belly
And he fell right to the floor.
Yes, I shot him in the belly
And he fell right to the floor.
Didn't want my man to suffer
so I shot him five times more.

The Moral

So girls, lissen to Big Sadie
and your life will turn out fine.
Yes girls, lissen to Big Sadie
and your life will turn out fine.
Don't take your man to Memphis –
you can buy that couch on-line.

L.A. L.A.

Author's Note

LA doesn't have a song.
New York has several songs. Chicago has a song. San Francisco has a song. But LA doesn't have a song.
I decided to write one.
I needed a tune. I decided to steal the tune from New York New York.
I figured no one would notice.

I'm taking a walk
Through downtown L.A.,
Because I found a parking spot
Eight blocks away.

You won't hear me squawk.
It's my lucky day,
Because I found a place to park
Where you don't pay.

I love to be here in the city that loves to drive.
The place where getting to work
Takes 9 to 5.

Yes, Frisco's got fog;
Chicago — the lake.
But if you want to live there that's
A big mistake.

L.A.'s the only place to be.
I love that air that I can see.
The smog is free
In wee
L.A.

A Real Sincere Country and Western Love Song

Author's Note
Strong Language Warning

This song contains the word "fuck".
If the word "fuck" offends you, perhaps it would be better if you did not read any further, because the word "fuck" is right there in the second stanza.

Well I sold my horse and saddle,
And I sold my pickup truck.
I sold off almost ev'rything in sight.

I don't need all those possessions.
Honey, I don't give a fuck.
If you will only sleep with me tonight.

All our cares will be forgotten,
In the glow of sweet romance.
I know that ev'rything will be alright.

So just lie down here beside me –
Let me get into your pants.
O my darlin', won't you sleep with me tonight.

The Cyclist's Song

Author's Note

I wrote this song while riding a bicycle.
I was on a bicycle tour in England. The tour company provided a support van that trailed us. In the event of an injury, or equipment failure, or heavy rain, we waited for the van to catch up with us and we got in the van.

The tune for the song is "Strike Up The Band"
The first eight lines are the introduction.
The remainder of the song is sung to the tune that is familiar to most people.

The cyclists' life's a healthy one
Up at the crack of dawn
There's lots of cycling to be done
Over the hill and yon
But there's one rule that we observe
That keeps us fit and nimble
At ev'ning time we're full of verve
The rule is oh so simple

If the rain goes splat
If your tire goes flat
Don't know where you're at
Get in the van

If the going's rough
If you've had enough
Lunch was awfully tough
Get in the van

But
If the hill's going down going down
And it's only a mile to town
Ride it out with a grin not a frown
Be a man

But if skies are grey
Feeling tired today
Don't fight it
Get it the van

Plays

I love plays. When I was a teenager I never read novels. I read plays. I read them out loud and acted out all of the parts. It was fun. Eventually I started writing plays. But, since my attention span is very short, my plays were short — one page, two pages. And in my rewrite of Hamlet, sixteen pages. How much does a playwright need?

Michelangelo Misunderstands The Instructions

Pope Julius: So, Michelangelo, you've locked yourself in the chapel for two years. When will it be finished?

Michelangelo: It's done. I finished it today. Would you like to see it?

Julius: Of course!

They enter the chapel.

Julius: What's ... all ... this ... scribbling?

Michelangelo: It's poetry. Sestinas. One thousand four hundred and sixty of them. That's two a day for two years. I just finished today. The whole world will marvel at the ceiling of the Sestina Chapel!

Julius: I wanted pictures, not poetry!!

Michelangelo: Pictures??

Julius: Pictures!!

Michelangelo: Not poetry??

Julius: Pic-tures!!

Michelangelo: (*Crushed*) Alright.
(*Recovering quickly*) Alright. Give me another week and you'll have it.

After The Fall

Author's Note

A friend of mine was telling me about her son who dropped out of college and decided to go out on his own. He wasn't sure what he wanted to do, but he wanted to be independent. I realized: that's what the Garden of Eden story is really about. There is no snake. When children are young, their parents provide for them. Eventually, they grow up, and they want to leave the home of their parents. Eventually, we all leave the Garden of Eden.

Adam and Eve have been expelled from the Garden of Eden. They are wandering in the woods outside of the garden when they come across five couples sitting on logs next to a pond. They approach.

Adam: Excuse me. I'm Adam and this is Eve. We've never seen other people before. Do you live here?

1st Man: We all live here. Where are you coming from?

Adam: We were living in the Garden of Eden, but we were thrown out.

1st Woman: Why?

Adam: We ate the Apple of Knowledge.

1st Man: Oh, another one.

Eve: Were you in the Garden of Eden?

1st Woman: We were all in the Garden of Eden and we were all thrown out.

Eve: Why?

1st Man: We were thrown out for eating the Banana of Knowledge.

2nd Man: We were thrown out for eating the Apricot of Knowledge.

3rd Woman: We were thrown out for eating the Mango of Knowledge.

4th Woman: We ate the Papaya of Knowledge. You can guess what happened.

5th Man: I went for a walk in the garden and Harriet made a salad. When I came back we ate it. A half hour later there was thunder and lightening and a booming voice told us that we had eaten the Apple of Knowledge, the Walnuts of Knowledge, the Celery of Knowledge, and the Mayonnaise of Knowledge. Then he threw us out.

Eve: Why does he do that?

5th Man: I don't know. He's always making up some reason.

Adam: But why?

5th Man: Don't you get it? It doesn't matter what you do. You're always going to be thrown out of the Garden of Eden.

Adam: Oh.

Long pause while Adam thinks it over.

94

Adam: What do you do for food here?

1st Man: Oh, there's lots of food here. It's not as good as the Garden of Eden, but it's good enough. You see these green stems here? You pull them up. This orange thing on the bottom is pretty good. It's crunchy and tasty. Here, try it.

Adam takes a bite.

Adam: It is good. What do you call it?

1st Man: I call it a carrot. Actually, I call it the Carrot of Ignorance.

Adam: Why do you call it that?

1st Man: I'm playing it safe. I don't want to get thrown out again.

The Day They Wrote The Bible

Characters:
Prophet   A tall man with a dramatic voice
Editor   A small man with a nasal voice. The Editor speaks slowly and enunciates each word carefully.

Editor: So, how's the writing going?

Prophet: Great! It all came to me in a dream last night.

Editor: That's good. I'm glad to hear it. So what do you have?

Prophet: I have a complete, coherent ethical framework. It's great.

Editor: That's good. So tell me more about it.

Prophet: I have ten basic principles that tell each person how to live their life.

Editor: That's good. So is there a story to go with it?

Prophet: Of course there's a story. It's the story of how these principles were handed down to us.

Editor: That's good. And there are characters in this story?

Prophet: Of course. This is a story about Man and his relationship with God.

Editor: That's good. A little sparse, but still, always a popular theme. So these principles — you have a few examples?

Prophet: (*Proudly*) "Thou shalt not kill"

Editor: (*Unimpressed*) Hmmm. You have any others?

Prophet: "Thou shalt not commit adultery"

Editor: That's good. I like that. A little controversial. I always said you were a good writer.

Prophet: It's not my writing. This is divinely inspired.

Editor: Of course. So you have this story, and this relationship, and these principles, and, uh, that's it?

Prophet: Yes. This is an ethical framework that will last forever. What more is there to say?

Editor: Do yourself a favor. Throw in a few miracles.

Prophet: Miracles? What do miracles have to do with this? This is about ethics!

Editor: Trust me. I've been doing this for a long time. Add a few miracles here and there. Perhaps a forest fire in the middle of a desert.

Prophet: But, this message, these principles, this ethic will last for all time. It doesn't need miracles to communicate it.

Editor: Look, you want this to be an all-time best seller. Right?

Prophet: What I want doesn't matter. It's God's will.

Editor: Of course. So don't disappoint Him. Add a few miracles and it will be in print for thousands of years.

Prophet: You think it will make that much of a difference?

Editor: Trust me. Ethics, philosophy, it doesn't sell that well. But add a few miracles and you'll be on top of the best seller list for 150,000 weeks.

Gertrude or Hamlet Improved

Author's Note

Rewriting Hamlet — it's irresistible. And it's easy. Everyone knows the characters. You just have to give them new words to say. In this version, Hamlet's mother, Gertrude, is the central character. Hamlet plays a secondary role.

Gertrude was performed, to great acclaim, at the Tom Nicotera Theater.[4]

Characters:

Gertrude	*The Queen of Denmark*
Claudius	*The King of Denmark*
Hamlet	*The Prince of Denmark*
Polonius	*Advisor to the Queen*
Ophelia	*The Ingénue of Denmark; Daughter of Polonius*
Laertes	*Son of Polonius*

---

[4] The Tom Nicotera Theater is located in Tom Nicotera's living room. From time to time, Tom invites many of his writer friends to come and perform their work. Sometimes it's poetry, sometimes plays, and in one case it was juggling while reciting an original poem. It's a grand occasion.

Scene 1
Gertrude and Hamlet

Gertrude: Hamlet, my son, you're always brooding these days. What is troubling you?

Hamlet: It's my father's death.

Gertrude: My son, it troubles all of us. It was so sudden, without warning. He was so filled with vitality and then he was gone.

Hamlet: And your marriage to his brother, Claudius.

Gertrude: That was not my idea, Hamlet. It is written in the Bible. If a man dies and leaves a widow, then his brother marries the widow. I did not write that. I'll show you.
(picks up a bible)
Here it is. "The Bible", written by: GOD

See? It wasn't my idea.

Hamlet: Mother, the Bible says that the brother must marry the widow if she has no male heir. I am the male heir.

Gertrude: Oops. Too late now. Forgive me, Hamlet. I didn't know about that technicality. I'm just a simple Queen, unschooled in these theological matters.

Hamlet: Mother, I wonder if Claudius had something to do with my father's death. He was always filled with envy. I saw the way he looked at you.

Gertrude: I saw it too. But what makes you so suspicious of Claudius?

Hamlet: I've seen a ghost.

Gertrude: A ghost?

Hamlet: Yes. A ghost. It may have been my father.

Gertrude: Hamlet, my son, do you know how long the royal family of Denmark has lived in this castle? Over 800 years! The palace is crawling with ghosts. What makes you think it was your father? Did it look like him?

Hamlet: Well, no. I couldn't tell. But he spoke to me.

Gertrude: What did he say?

Hamlet: He said: "Remember me."

Gertrude: They all say that. They're dead and they think they've been forgotten. They walk through the halls at night and when they meet someone they say: "Hello. Remember me?"

Hamlet: But he said more.

Gertrude: What more did he say?

Hamlet: He said:
"I could a tale unfold whose lightest word
Would harrow up thy soul, freeze thy young blood,
Make thy two eyes, like stars, start from their spheres,
Thy knotted and combined locks to part
And each particular hair to stand on end."

Gertrude: (*shakes her head*)
That doesn't sound like your father. Too wordy. He was much
more a man of action. More like:
(*mimics his gruff voice*) "You! Here! Do this! Now! Or else!"
He was not an easy man to live with.

Hamlet: But he spoke of being murdered – and revenge.

Gertrude: Hamlet, my son, do you think your father was the
only king who ever died suddenly?
Pause
Still, it's possible.
Another pause
But you're too young to be brooding and filled with thoughts of
revenge. Your life should be filled with joy.
Let me take care of this for you. I'll look into it. And if I find out
that Claudius murdered your father, I'll poison him myself. He
trusts me. It will be easy.

Meanwhile, you should be enjoying yourself. All of these
young ladies of the court have eyes for you. You could have
your pick.

Hamlet: I'm not in the mood.

Gertrude: Then change your mood to a lighter one. Haven't you
noticed the beautiful Ophelia? She blushes whenever she sees
you. I'm a woman and I know about these things. I'll bet she
wets her pants whenever you walk by. That is, she would, if she
wore underpants. Spend some time with her. I'm sure she'll
raise your spirits.

Hamlet: I'll try, mother.

Scene 2
Gertrude and Ophelia

Gertrude: My sweet Ophelia, my son Hamlet is troubled these days. He needs your help, and so do I.

Ophelia: Your majesty, I will gladly do whatever you ask of me.

Gertrude: Spend time with him. Lead him away from troubled thoughts. Turn him toward happier thoughts. Raise his spirits — if you get my drift.

Ophelia: I would gladly do that. But I don't know what to do. I smile at him whenever I see him, but he never seems to notice me.

Gertrude: Men are sometimes like that. You must be sly about it. Perhaps if you tripped, and your dress flew up over your head. I'm sure he would notice that.

Ophelia: How clever you are. I'll do it the next time I see him.

Gertrude: You know, my sweet Ophelia, I've always thought that you and my son would make a perfect match. It would make me very happy to see the two of you together.

Ophelia: Oh, thank you, your majesty.

Gertrude: And you don't have to call me "Your Majesty". Just call me ... Mom.

Scene 3

Gertrude and Polonius

Gertrude: Polonius, old friend, dear friend. How much I have counted on you all these years. Your wise counsel and your wit and your silver tongue, your eloquence. You have guided me through many difficult moments. And now, this most troublesome situation. The court is filled with rumors and suspicion. I need your help, old friend. Can I count on you?

Polonius: *Nods.*
Uh-huh.

Gertrude: I knew I could. Now, I must ask you do something special for me. I ask you to silence that silver tongue of yours. Silence. Say nothing to anyone. Say nothing to Claudius. Say nothing to Hamlet. Say nothing to Ophelia and Laertes. Whatever happens, say nothing. Can I count on you to do that?

Polonius: *Nods.*
Uh-huh.

Gertrude: Thank you old friend. I know you will never betray me.
(Harshly) You know, I would hate to see that silver tongue of yours on a delicatessen platter.
(Sweetly) But what am I saying? I know you will never betray me. Thank you old friend. Thank you.

Polonius: *Starts to speak*

Gertrude: Silence!

Polonius: *Nods.*
Uh-huh.

Scene 4
Gertrude and Laertes

Gertrude: Laertes, I have known you since you were a child, a bright and beautiful child. And now, you have grown into a brave and handsome young man. Your father, Polonius, has taught you well, and now you are wise beyond your years.

Laertes: Thank you, your majesty.

Gertrude: The King is very impressed with you. He looks upon you with favor.

Laertes: It is a great honor, your majesty.

Gertrude: You know, Laertes, it is said that there is a time for speaking out and there is a time for discretion. Tell me Laertes, what time is it now?

Laertes: It is a time for discretion, your majesty.

Gertrude: Well spoken, Laertes.

Laertes: Thank you, your majesty.

Gertrude: Laertes, I would like you to do some community service. This is to be a surprise for the King, so don't tell him about it. There is a nunnery nearby. In it are a number of beautiful young ladies who have had the misfortune to make a small mistake early in life. Spend some time with them. Get to know them. Counsel them. Show them compassion. *(Slowly)* Take your time.
Can you do that for me?

Laertes: Yes, your majesty. When would you like me to leave?

Gertrude: Now. Get thee to the nunnery. And don't come back for a week.

Laertes: Yes, your majesty.

Gertrude: And you don't have to call me "Your Majesty". Just call me ... Gertrude the Great

Scene 5

Gertrude is alone

Gertrude: Ah, me. What am I to do?
Shall I be Monarch or simply the Queen?

How much simpler it was when King Hamlet was alive.
I was so happy to be his Queen.
To sit next to him and admire his manliness.
To cheer him up after a hard day of scowling.
I wanted nothing more than to please him.
I even took Chinese cooking lessons.
I made a special dinner for him.
Alas, by accident, I poisoned him.

Pause

Life can be terribly cruel.
True, he was not the ideal husband.
Anyone who takes a sword to bed is not what you would call a romantic.
Still, I loved him.
 (Sadly) And now he is gone.

Pause

(Brightly) Oh, well, live and learn I always say.

Now, if Claudius were to die, there would be no more brothers to marry and I would become the Monarch.
It would be a heavy burden.
But would it not be better for Denmark?
To be led by a woman?
A woman who would use tact and diplomacy rather than war?
And not just any woman.
Me!

What is it to be?
Shall I be Monarch or simply the Queen?

Pause

I think I'll be Monarch.

Scene 6
Gertrude and Claudius

Gertrude: Claudius, my darling. Let's have dinner.

Claudius: I'd love to. But, where is everybody?

Gertrude: The last I saw of Hamlet, he was chasing Ophelia though the castle.

Claudius: And Laertes?

Gertrude: He's off doing charity work. He's such a fine fellow.

Claudius: Indeed, he is. And where is Polonius?

Gertrude: I asked him to open a few windows. It's so stuffy in here.

Claudius: Where is the food taster?

Gertrude: That vulture! He's doubled in size since he came here. Someone should tell that there's a difference between tasting and gulping.
Anyway, he asked to be excused. He said he had an upset stomach.

It's just the two of us, Claudius. I prefer it this way, don't you? It gives us a chance to have an intimate dinner without distractions.
I made it myself. Just for you.

Do you like Chinese food?

Claudius: Chinese food? I don't know. I've never tried it.

Gertrude: Trust me, darling. You'll love it. It's to die for.

Scene 7

The Next Morning
Claudius is dead
The food taster is dead

Gertrude, Hamlet, and Ophelia

Hamlet: Mother, something wonderful has happened. I've fallen in love. Lately, I've been feeling so down. Then, somehow everything changed. My world turned upside down. And then I saw Ophelia, as if for the first time.
(Ophelia winks at the Queen)
My heart is filled with love for Ophelia.

Gertrude: And you, sweet Ophelia? Do you share Hamlet's feelings?

(Ophelia looks at Hamlet lovingly and flutters her eyelashes)
Ophelia: Oh yes! I've loved Hamlet all along. I'm head-over-heels about him.

Gertrude: Then it's decided! We will make preparations for a splendid wedding for the two of you.

Hamlet: We must tell the King.

Gertrude: Alas, Claudius is dead. Someone left the window open and Claudius caught a sudden Winter cold. How deadly those colds can be and how swift. First the coughing, then the coffin.

So I am now the Monarch.
We're going to have a busy social season.
The funeral, the wedding, the coronation.

But you needn't concern yourself with these matters.
You two lovers, go off and celebrate your happiness.
I'll take care of these silly affairs of state.

Hamlet: Thank you, Mother.

Ophelia: Thanks, Mom

Hamlet and Ophelia leave

Scene 8
Gertrude and Polonius

Gertrude: Polonius, old friend, help me!
Claudius is dead and I am now the Monarch.
What am I to do? A great army is massing to the north of us.
When the Spring comes they will invade, conquer Denmark,
and destroy the Monarchy. That's me, you know. What am I to
do? Speak to me old friend. Advise me.

Polonius:
Your highness,
To expostulate what majesty should be, what duty is,
Why day is day, night night, and time is time,
Were nothing but to waste night, day and time.
Therefore, since brevity is the soul of wit,
And tediousness the limbs and outward flourishes,
I will be brief.

Gertrude: (*rolls her eyes*)
Enough!
I'll figure it out myself.

Scene 9
A Month Later
Gertrude is now the Monarch.
She sits alone and muses about matters of state.

Gertrude: Young Fortinbras is leading his army to conquer Denmark. I must avoid war. I must use diplomacy. We must become friends. After all, we are one people. The bad feelings of the past must be swept away. All those who killed long ago are gone. The slate is clean.

I will invite him to the palace. No need for armies. He shall be our guest. We will welcome him with open arms. We will have a feast in his honor.

Pause

I wonder if he likes Chinese food?

The End

Macbeth

A ONE-MINUTE MUSICAL

Author's Note

It's been 50 years since I read Macbeth. I couldn't remember the story. All I could remember was there is a "Tomorrow and tomorrow and tomorrow'" speech and somewhere Lady Macbeth says "Out damned spot". But that's all I needed. After all, the entire play has to be performed in one minute.

Tragedy is very iffy. I think turning Macbeth into a musical ensured its success.

Repeating the performance in mime, as a silent musical, showed just how avant-garde we could be.

Macbeth was performed at the Tom Nicotera Theater to pretty good acclaim.

Characters:
Lady Macbeth
Macbeth
Backup Singer(s)
A Narrator
A Shill in the audience

Narrator: The One-Minute Theater Company presents:
Macbeth — The Musical

Lady Macbeth and Macbeth

Macbeth is seated, sleeping.

Lady Macbeth: (*Shakes Macbeth's shoulder and wakes him*)
Macbeth, I'm tired seeing you sleeping all day. Go out and get a job!

Macbeth: I'll do it tomorrow.

Lady Macbeth: Tomorrow and tomorrow and tomorrow.
That's all I ever hear from you.
Don't you have any ambition?
Look, here's a want ad. Wanted: Thane of Cawdor.
No experience necessary.
You can do that job. Go out and talk to them!

Macbeth: Alright. Alright. I'll do it.

Lady Macbeth: And take the dog for a walk. He's been waiting all day.
(*Calls the dog*) Spot! Out!
(*Mutters*) Damn dog.

The back-up singers sing "Get a Job".
The curtain falls
The End
The audience applauds.
Someone (a shill) shouts "Encore"

The members of the cast confer with each other.

Narrator: The One-Minute Theater Company presents:
Macbeth — The Musical — Silent Movie Version

The cast performs Macbeth, mimes the same dialogue, makes exaggerated gestures.
The Backup Singer(s) mime the words to "Get a Job".

The Heimlich Maneuver

AUTHOR'S NOTE

The Heimlich Maneuver is a play that is so sexually explicit that it is best if it is performed in total darkness — including the curtain calls.

Characters:
The Narrator
Dr. Henry Heimlich
Jane

Narrator: The One Minute Theater Company presents:
"The Heimlich Maneuver"

For a few moments there is silence. Then…

Jane: Oh, Dr. Heimlich.

Dr. Heimlich: Call me Henry.

Jane: Henry, I love the way you touch me.

Jane: Oh… Oh…

Jane: What are you doing?

What follows is a crescendo of moans and cries of passion, followed by heavy breathing, gasping for air, etc. The actor playing Jane should feel free to improvise.

Jane: Oh…Oh… Oh… That was wonderful. I never felt anything like that.
Where did you learn to do that?

Dr. Heimlich: I invented it.

Short pause

Jane: Really? *Longer pause*   Do it again.

Narrator: The End

The actors come onstage and take a bow.

About The Author

Shelly Weinberg has been a featured poet at Bethel, Norwich, and Wintonbury, Connecticut. He has also read at a number of other Connecticut venues.

Shelly has been hanging around with poets for a number of years. Inspired by their artistry he decided to devote himself to the mastery of poetic forms. Sonnet, villanelle, haiku, double dactyl, limerick, free verse, plays, essays, and songs – he has worked with all of them. His work has been so well received that he has decided to publish it anyway.

The turning point in Shelly's writing career came when his internist advised him to lose weight. Shelly quit his job and has subsisted entirely on his earnings from poetry. He's lost fifteen pounds so far.